SCHOLASTIC
Phonics

AF072339

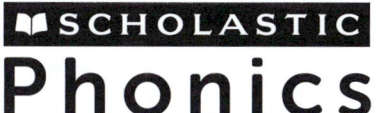

Land Meets Sea

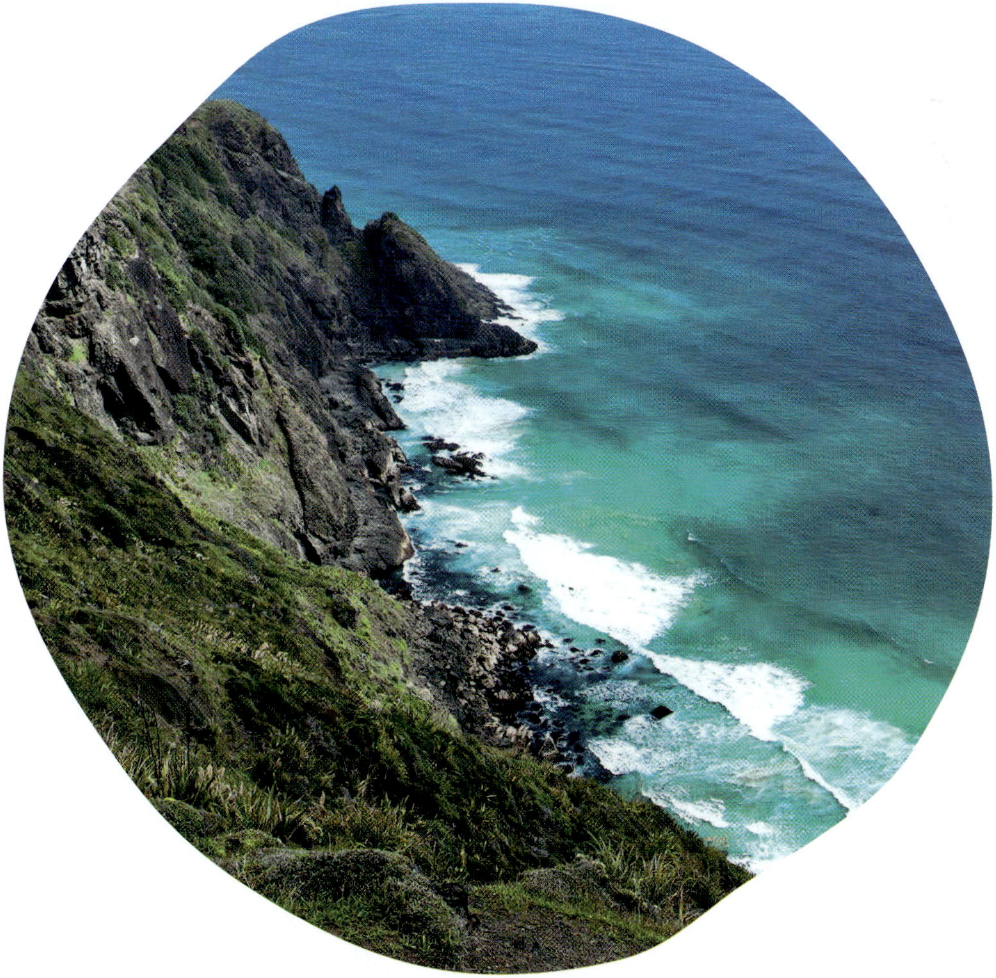

Published in the UK by Scholastic Education, 2023
Scholastic Distribution Centre, Bosworth Avenue, Tournament Fields, Warwick, CV34 6UQ
Scholastic Ireland, 89E Lagan Road, Dublin Industrial Estate, Glasnevin, Dublin, D11 HP5F

SCHOLASTIC and associated logos are trademarks and/or registered trademarks of Scholastic Inc.
www.scholastic.co.uk
© 2023 Scholastic
1 2 3 4 5 6 7 8 9   3 4 5 6 7 8 9 0 1 2

Printed by Ashford Colour Press
The book is made of materials from well-managed, FSC®-certified forests and other controlled sources.

A CIP catalogue record for this book is available from the British Library.
ISBN 978-0702-32102-3

All rights reserved. This book is sold subject to the condition that it shall not, by way of trade or otherwise, be lent, hired out or otherwise circulated in any form of binding or cover other than that in which it is published. No part of this publication may be reproduced, stored in a retrieval system, or transmitted in any form or by any other means (electronic, mechanical, photocopying, recording or otherwise) without prior written permission of Scholastic.

Every effort has been made to trace copyright holders for the works reproduced in this publication, and the publishers apologise for any inadvertent omissions.

Author
Rachel Russ

Editorial team
Rachel Morgan, Vicki Yates, Alison Gilbert, Jennie Clifford

Design team
Dipa Mistry, Andrea Lewis, We Are Grace

Photographs
Cover no_limit_pictures/iStock
p1, 4–5 Arcanion/Shutterstock
p6–7 Andy333/Shutterstock
p8 Sascha Burkard/Shutterstock
p9 William Reynolds/iStock
p10 Aoosthuizen/iStock
p11 Dgwildlife/iStock
p12–13 tirc83/iStock
p14 Try Media/iStock
p3, 15 davemantel/iStock
p16, 24 AlasdairJames/iStock
p17 Victoria Gardner/iStock
p18 Elena_Alex_Ferns/Shutterstock
p19, 24 2009fotofriends/Shutterstock
p20 Wirestock/iStock
p21, 24 Martin Prochazkacz/Shutterstock
p22–23 Aleh Varanishcha/iStock

Help your child to read!

This book practises these letters and letter sounds.
Point and say the sounds with your child:

- ay (as in 'ways')
- ou (as in 'out')
- ea (as in 'sea')
- ir (as in 'birds')
- ie (as in 'tries')

Your child may need help to read these common tricky words:

- the
- have
- to
- here
- by
- of
- one
- so
- comes
- are
- like
- be
- they
- when

Before reading
- Look at the cover picture and read the title together. Read the back cover blurb to your child.
- Ask your child: *Have you been to the coast? What did you see there?*
- Talk about the image in the magnifying glass.

During reading
- If your child gets stuck on a word, remind them to sound it out and then blend the sounds to read the word: l-ie, lie.
- If they are still stuck, show them how to read the word.
- Enjoy looking at the pictures together. Pause to talk about the information.

After reading
- Talk about the images on page 24. What can your child tell you about them?
- Ask your child: *How do creatures in a rock pool avoid getting washed away by the sea?*
- Discuss which page your child found most interesting or surprising.

The Coast

At the coast, the land meets the sea.

cliffs

beach

Birds, seals and fish have found clever ways to stay here.

Cliffs

Steep cliffs get battered by the wind and sea spray.

Yet lots of seabirds nest here!

Bigger birds that eat seabirds cannot reach them.

The puffin tries to nest underground near cliffs.

It can nest in cracks in the cliffs too!

Puffins lay one egg each year.

The puffling (chick) first flies away in the dark so it is not spied by bigger birds.

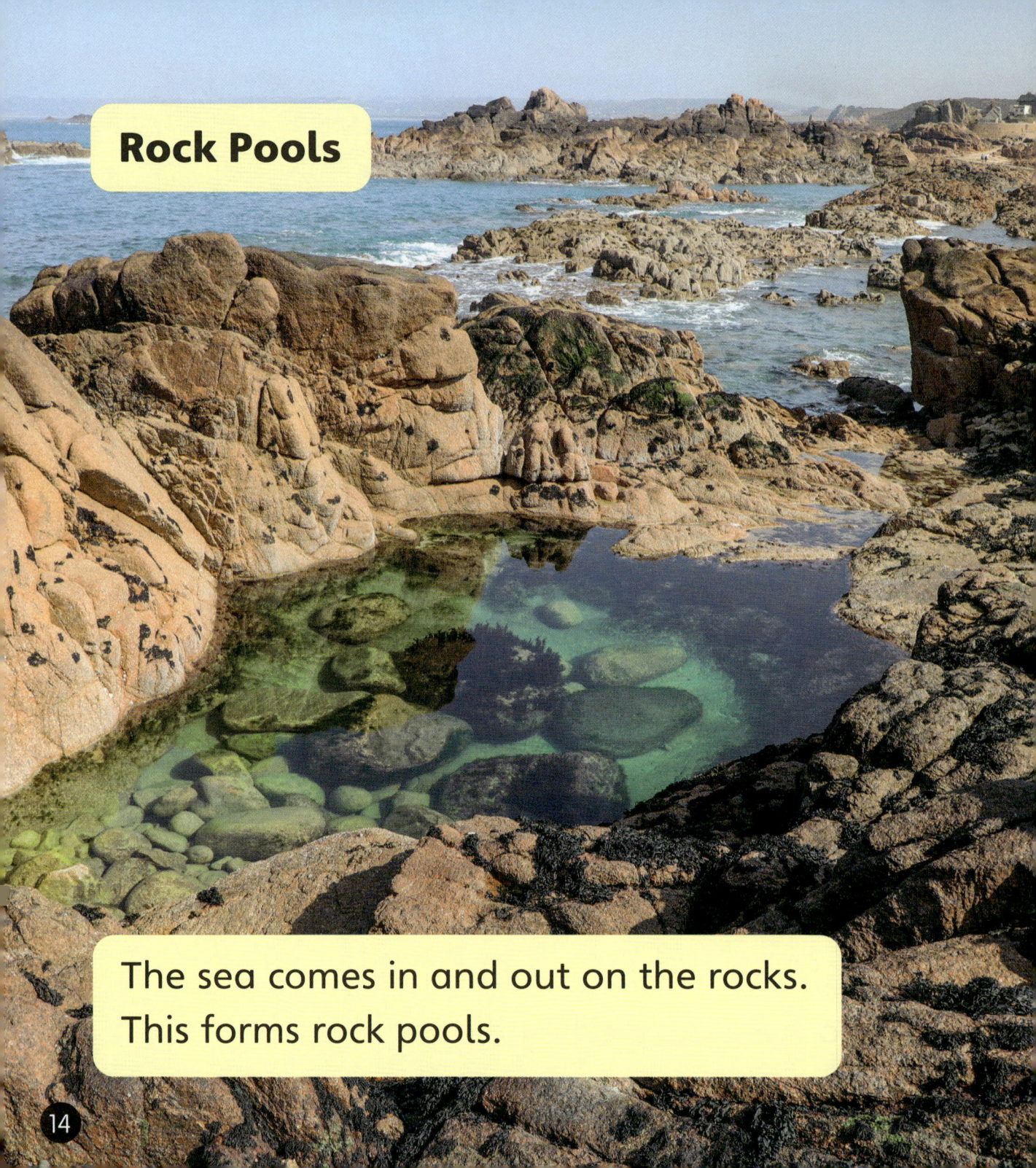

Rock Pools

The sea comes in and out on the rocks. This forms rock pools.

Fish, crabs and seaweed are found here.

Starfish have lots of suckers to grip to rocks like glue.

crab

Crabs lurk in cracks in the rock.
The sea cannot sweep them away.

On the Beach

On the beach, birds gather in flocks.

Dunlins have long, thin beaks to pluck insects out of the wet sand.

Seals can be in the sea and on land. They hunt for fish in the sea.

When they have had a meal, they lie and rest on the beach.

For birds, seals, crabs and starfish, the coast is a perfect habitat.

Talk about it!